CONTEMPORARY INTROITS

CONTEMPORARY INTROITS
for the Revised Church Calendar

Leslie F. Brandt

Publishing House
St. Louis

Concordia Publishing House, St. Louis, Missouri
Copyright © 1975 Concordia Publishing House
MANUFACTURED IN THE UNITED STATES OF AMERICA

Library of Congress Cataloging in Publication Data

Brandt, Leslie F
    Contemporary introits for the revised Church calendar.

    1. Introits. I. Title.
BX8067.I57B7   264'.04'1   75-25525
ISBN 0-570-03718-2

CONTENTS

Preface 7
Introits for the Church Year 9
Alternate and Special Introits 30

PREFACE

The *Contemporary Introits and Collects* previously published (C. S. S. Publishing Co., Lima, Ohio) apparently meet a need and are in use in many congregations. I have been requested to extend them and attempt to relate them to the revised church calendar. I have endeavored to do this with the Introits alone. I have not been concerned about matching them up with particular texts of Scripture, but I have attempted to relate them to Sundays and seasons of the church year. In addition are included a larger number of alternate or special Introits that may be useful.

The Collects, or Prayers of the Day, are written by the Subcommittee on Prayers (of which I was a member) of the Inter-Lutheran Commission on Worship and are included in the "Propers" section of *Contemporary Worship 6: The Church Year Calendar and Lectionary*, which has been published by the ILCW.

Many of the Introits herein are portions of the contemporary psalms that I wrote and which are published by Concordia Publishing House in a volume titled *Psalms/Now*.

Leslie F. Brandt

INTROITS
FOR THE CHURCH YEAR

First Sunday in Advent

Praise God! As long as we have breath in our bodies, we will praise God! He who created the earth and all that abides upon it, He is that One who can heal the wounds and mend the fractures of this disjointed world. He can break the bonds of obsession and pierce man's stupor with visions of truth. He tenderly reaches out to those who are oppressed and reveals His concern for those who are lost and lonely. He watches over His own while the paths of the godless lead to their own destruction. This is the God revealed to us through the Christ of Christmas. This is the God who has come to us. Praise God! Amen.

Second Sunday in Advent

Now hear this, all who seek God! What the prophets of old promised and the people of Israel anticipated, has happened. The kingdom of God has come! God is here! Let us rejoice because He is present here with us! Let us break forth in shouts of praise and songs of joy! Listen, O God, to our songs of thanksgiving and respond to the hearts that reach out for You today. Amen.

Third Sunday in Advent

Delight yourselves in the Lord; find your joy in Him in all seasons. Never forget that He is in our midst, that He is very near to us every hour of each day. And this means that we need not worry over anything and need only tell

Him our every desire in earnest and thankful prayer. O God, You have blessed our lives with abundance. You have come to us and delivered us from eternal bondage. You have reunited us to Your family. We are Yours forever. Praises be to our great and loving God. Amen.

Fourth Sunday in Advent

The Word became flesh and dwelled in our midst. We have seen His glory and splendor. And from Him we have received abundant grace. No one has ever seen God, but His only Son has come to make Him known to us. Blessed be our God who has revealed Himself to us through Jesus Christ. Amen.

The Nativity of our Lord (Christmas Day)

We could not come to Him, so our great God has come to us. He made Himself known to our world through His Son. He has broken through the darkness and distortion of our sin. He has prepared a way of salvation for us. He came by way of the stable and the manger and the womb of woman, but He came to be our Savior and King. Let us sing our praises unto God, for He has done a marvelous and miraculous thing in our midst! Amen.

First Sunday After Christmas

God has come; He is here. Let us celebrate! With song and with dance, with stringed instruments and brass, with cymbals and drums, let us express our ecstatic joy in God's presence! Let us celebrate with the old songs of praise; let us also create new songs that portray the eternal love of our God! He created this world. He continues to permeate it with His love. Even amongst its distortions, its frustrated and unbelieving children, He constantly carries out

His purposes. He continues to reign over us and to reveal Himself to us. God is, indeed, in our midst, and this is cause for celebration. Amen.

The Name of Jesus

Blessed be the name of our Lord. Blessed be the name of Jesus through whom our great God revealed Himself to us. It is in the name of Jesus that we claim our salvation; it is in His name that we go forth to proclaim the Gospel and gather a people for Him. May His name be upon our lips and His Spirit in our hearts as we, in word and deed, seek to communicate His life and salvation to the multitudes about us. Blessed be the name of Jesus. Amen.

Second Sunday After Christmas

We know that our God has come and that He is here. We know this because when we laid bare our souls and stood naked before Him, He mercifully looked upon us with love and responded to our cries for help. We know this because He came to us through His Son, our Lord. We are the sons and daughters of our God, the servants and disciples of Jesus Christ, and we shall love Him forever. Amen.

The Epiphany of Our Lord

Our almighty and everywhere-present God is in our world. His majesty is reflected in creation about us; His love is revealed through the Christ who has come to us. And yet there are multitudes who do not feel His concern or acknowledge His love. God forbid that we be deaf to the cries of the poor and indifferent to those who have needs. May we identify with those who are oppressed and help to bear the burdens of those who suffer about us. God grant that they hear His voice of concern and feel His loving touch through His servants about them. The glory is Yours, O God, and we shall praise Your name and celebrate Your presence forever. Amen.

The Baptism of Our Lord ## *(First Sunday After Epiphany)*

Our heavenly Father, who gave His Spirit to His Son and who commissioned Him at His baptism to carry out the eternal purposes of God and bring His salvation to the inhabitants of this world, has now made us the objectives of His everlasting love and commissioned us to carry on His purposes in our world. He gave us His Spirit at our baptism; He has entrusted us to be His servants in our world today. We praise our God for His love for His children. We pray that we may be faithful to Him and His will for our lives. Amen.

Second Sunday After Epiphany

God is here—let's celebrate! Let us enlist our lives in perpetual celebration over God's goodness and greatness! Let us announce to the world God's presence and proclaim His loving concern for all men! How incomparably glorious is our great God! May our mouths articulate and our lives demonstrate His ever-present love for all the creatures of our world. Let us celebrate the eternal mercy and goodness of our God! Amen.

Third Sunday After Epiphany

The Lord is our constant companion. There is no need that He cannot fulfill. Whether His course for us points to the mountaintops of glorious ecstasy or the the valleys of human misery, He is by our side; He is ever present with us. When the pain is severe, He is near to comfort. When the burden is heavy, He is there to lean upon. When depression darkens our souls, He touches us with eternal joy. When we feel empty and alone, He fills the aching vacuum with His presence and power. This is the God we worship today. Amen.

Fourth Sunday After Epiphany

Our hearts overflow with gratitude to our God. We feel so exuberant that we simply must give expression or explode. We will give voice to our exultations. We will sing the praises of our God. Let us proclaim loudly His deeds to the people! For while He judges evildoers, He hears and remembers the cries of those in distress. Blessed be our loving God. Amen.

Fifth Sunday After Epiphany

Our God is the Creator and Performer of great and glorious things. There is no one like Him. He has kept us amidst life's conflicts, led us through its crucible of experiences, and drawn us back from its pitfalls and precipices. And He has healed our wounds and comforted us amidst our afflictions. Thus we know that He will continue to love and care for us forever. Amen.

Sixth Sunday After Epiphany

It is time we begin to make joyful noises about God, that we boldly proclaim His name and shout His praises. He draws us into the crucible of conflict; He tests and tries us in the valley of pain and sorrow; He allows us to taste the agony of affliction; He gives our enemies permission to oppose and oppress us. And then He uses these very things to purge and prepare us for His purposes. It is time we begin to make joyful noises about God, that we boldly proclaim His name and shout His praises. Amen.

Seventh Sunday After Epiphany

Our almighty and eternal God has always been God. Long before the earth was formed, long after it ceases to exist, He has been and He shall always be. He breaks into our short span of existence with His eternal love and grace. He brightens up our days of despair with hours of joy. He enables us to see something of His will and purpose for our creation and to discover some meaning for our brief and trouble-fraught appearance in this world. He imprints upon us His brand of ownership and places us within His plan and objective for our lives. We offer our praises to our almighty and eternal God. Amen.

Eighth Sunday After Epiphany

Our hearts are bursting with praises to God, every fiber of our beings reach out in rejoicing! How can we ever forget His many blessings? He forgives all our sins; He touches our afflictions with healing; He snatches us back from the gaping jaws of hell; He covers us with concern and love; He fulfills our deepest desires and gives us meaning for life and purpose for living. Our hearts are bursting with praises to God. Amen.

The Transfiguration of Our Lord
(Last Sunday After Epiphany)

How full of wonder and splendor is our God! We see the reflections of His beauty and hear the sounds of His majesty wherever we turn. Even the babbling of babes and the laughter of children spell out His name in indefinable syllables. When we gaze into star-studded skies and attempt to comprehend the vast distances, we contemplate in utter amazement our Creator's concern for us. We are dumbfounded that He should care about us. And yet He has made us in His image. He calls us His sons and daughters. He has ordained us as His priests and chosen us to be His servants. He has assigned to us the fantastic responsibility of carrying on His creative activity. How full of wonder and splendor is our God! Amen.

Ash Wednesday

We come to embrace the love and mercy of our gracious Lord. We have no security except in Him. We are perpetually exposed to the destructive forces of this existence. We are in constant danger of losing the battle to the very passions and desires of our sin-permeated natures. We can only submit ourselves to Him and believe that He will fulfill His purposes in us. The love of God is steadfast; His grace is everlasting. We shall sing His praises forever. Amen.

First Sunday in Lent

That one whose faith is focused on God, who finds his security in Him, does not have to live in fear. He is not left untouched by the tempests of this life, and he may be wounded by the onslaughts of evil, but our God does not leave him to suffer these things alone. The Lord cares for His own and delivers him even in the midst of the conflicts that plague him. This is our God whom we honor and adore today. He is in our midst, and we offer our praises to Him. Amen.

Second Sunday in Lent

We raise our voices in praise, O God, because no one can separate us from You. Though circumstances threaten us and our own obsessions entangle us, You will never let us go. Your great power is sufficient to set us free from these things that hurt our souls. If we put our trust in You, You will not allow them to destroy us. We thank You, our Lord, for we are Yours forever. Amen.

Third Sunday in Lent

We are reaching again for our God. From the abyss of defeat, the suffocating shame of failure, we seek His mercy and His help. He will enable us to see something of His will for our lives. He will break through this stifling darkness with some direction, some meaning, some purpose for our existence. He is our God; He has promised us salvation. We offer up our praises to Him. Amen.

Fourth Sunday in Lent

The faithful and the faithless both suffer the uncertainties and insecurities of this life, but the child of God can depend always on the love of his Father. It is for this reason that there is light even in the midst of darkness and incomprehensible joy in the midst of sorrow, and we can find a measure of happiness and well-being regardless of the circumstances that surround us. We sing the praises of our God. We celebrate His eternal love and concern for us. Amen.

Fifth Sunday in Lent

Does our God ever give us up? Does He remember the uncountable times we have failed Him? He reminds us of His steadfast love, that His concern is for those who fail and fumble; and He seeks incessantly to restore to Himself those who humbly reach out for Him. This is the God whom we worship; this is the God whom we praise. Amen.

Sunday of the Passion (Palm Sunday)

Let us look up and live! God is present in all His glory and majesty. Let us let go and celebrate! Our loving Lord is here with us and will manifest Himself through us. We are the vehicles and vessels of the King of kings. We represent Him in all His saving power. We are His beloved and empowered servants in this world that He created. We are His forever. Praise God! Amen.

Maundy Thursday

Our God does hear us when we cry out to Him. He does not ignore our needs, nor is He indifferent to our desires. He will not let us go even if the whole world should turn against us. He will sustain us and keep us on course even amongst the dangers and pitfalls of this life. It is this that spells out the greatness of God, and this is the God whom we worship today. Amen.

Good Friday

It is no wonder that we love our God. He has granted to us a security that we could never find among the things of this world. He has erased from our lives the fear of death. What follows the grave is not our fearful concern. The traumatic experiences of this life cannot destroy us. He is never out of reach but is ever aware of our problems and conflicts. It is no wonder that we love our God. Amen.

The Resurrection of Our Lord (Easter Day)

Our great God has raised His Son from the grave! Christ is alive! Christ is for real! He has arisen! And He is here today to share His resurrection with us. The same power that raised Jesus from the dead is available to us today. It has taken the fear out of death and reduced the might of our enemies to impotence. His victory is our victory. We shall live forever. May God be praised forever! Amen.

Second Sunday of Easter

Our loving God through the living Christ has turned our griping into gratitude, our screams of despair into proclamations of joy. Now we can explode with praises, and we will spend eternity in thanksgiving to our God. He is our hope and salvation. We will sing His praises forever. Amen.

Third Sunday of Easter

Break forth into exclamations of joy and gladness, you who serve the Lord! God is not dead! He is ever our God! He made us; we belong to Him; we are His sons and daughters. And His love for us never runs out; His care and concern for us will go on forever. Let the world see our manifestations of joy! Let us lift up our voices in songs of praise and surrender our lives as perpetual offerings of thanksgiving! Let us bless His name forever! Amen.

Fourth Sunday of Easter

Rejoice with me, you who are His invisible servants and you who hear and obey His voice! Shout His praises, you who are His children and you who serve as His ministers and priests! This is no time for despair and discouragement. Whoever and wherever you are, lift your hearts in praises to God. Amen.

Fifth Sunday of Easter

Clap your hands; stamp your feet! Let your bodies and your voices explode with joy. God is not some human concoction. He is for real! and He is here! Despite all attempts to rationalize Him out of existence, He is in our world; and He reigns over our universe. Let us recognize His presence and fill the air with His praises! Amen.

Sixth Sunday of Easter

It's a glorious feeling to be able to unload our hearts, to spill out our gratitude in thanks to our God. Morning, noon, and night, we want the whole world to know of His love. We want to shout it, to sing it, in every possible way to proclaim His praises, to express our joy. How great is our God! His thoughts are unfathomable, His ways beyond comprehension, His love is everlasting; and we are His forever. Amen.

The Ascension of Our Lord

There is no way to escape our God, no place to hide. If we ascend to the heights of joy, He is there before us. If we are plunged into the depths of despair, He is there to meet us. We could fly to the other side of our world and find Him there to lead the way. We could walk into the darkest of nights, only to find Him there to lighten its dismal hours. May our all-knowing, everywhere-present God search out our feelings and thoughts, deliver us from that which may hurt or destroy us, and guide us along the paths of love and truth. Amen.

Seventh Sunday of Easter

God is indeed in our world. From dawn to dusk, from twilight hours to the first light on eastern horizon, God is near us and around us. He speaks to our world; He speaks gently in love and thunders fiercely in judgment. He calls to those who are faithful to Him. He comforts them and challenges them; He secures them and sends them forth.

God is at work in our world. He works in and through the lives of His children who are loyal and obedient to Him. God is in our world. We serve Him with the kind of worship and thanksgiving that effectively communicates His love to His children in need about us. Amen.

The Day of Pentecost

We praise our loving God, the basis of all being and our ultimate and eternal concern. We know that He is not floating out there over and beyond our ball of clay. He is in our world. He took His Son from us only to return to us by way of His invisible Spirit. He is amongst His creatures, inscrutable, indefinable, great in majesty and splendor. He brings beauty out of ugliness. Out of the ashes of our sickness and suffering, He brings forth new creations of joy and loveliness. We shall never want to define You, O God, for we cannot worship what we comprehend. But we pray for Your grace to stand firm even in the midst of our nagging doubts and to praise You in the midst of adversity. Amen.

First Sunday After Pentecost (Trinity Sunday)

You well deserve the praises of Your children, O God. You make Your power known to us in the majestic grandeur of the mountains and in the thunderous roar of the ocean's waves. Your abundance is poured out upon us in the grain-laden fields, the flocks in the meadows, the gentle rain that caresses the green hills. Your love for us is manifested in Your Son, our Lord, Jesus Christ. Your presence with us is made known to us through Your Spirit. You well deserve the praises of Your children, O God. Amen.

Second Sunday After Pentecost

We feel like singing this morning. We feel like telling everyone about us about the greatness of our God. If only they could know the depths of His love and His eternal concern for those who will follow Him! Even the songs of the birds proclaim His praises. The heavens and the earth beneath them, the trees that reach toward the skies, the flowers that glow in colorful beauty, the green hills and soaring mountains, the valleys and the plains, the lakes and the rivers, the great oceans that pound our shores, they proclaim the greatness of our God and His love for the human family. How glorious it is to be alive! May every breath of our bodies, every beat of our hearts, be dedicated to the praise and glory of God! Amen.

Third Sunday After Pentecost

We celebrate God's blessings upon our world: the flowers that bloom in glorious color, the rains that freshen the earth, the birds that fill the air with song. We give thanks for His love for His children: His forgiveness of our sin, His pursuit of those who run from Him, His reaching out to heal them and to draw them to Himself. We call upon all men to praise the Lord: those who preach to proclaim His love, those who sing to glorify His name, those who can shout or whistle or write or paint or dance or play musical instruments or pound on drums or ring bells to join in celebrating the majesty and splendor of our great and loving God. Amen.

Fourth Sunday After Pentecost

How grateful we are to our God today! He is a merciful and loving God. How tenderly He deals with those whose hearts are open to Him! He is a righteous and faithful God.

His promises and precepts are forever. He is a majestic and powerful God. He created us and sustains us day by day. He is a forgiving God. He takes us back to His loving heart when we go astray. He is in this world today. And those who recognize and accept His presence are building on foundations that are eternally secure. How grateful we are to our God today. Amen.

Fifth Sunday After Pentecost

Our loving God reaches into our distraught lives to heal our wounds. He encompasses us with eternal love. He abides with us even in the midst of conflict or calamity. He sets us free from self-idolatry so we may serve His creatures about us. He shields us from the forces that are intent on our destruction. We are His delight and heart's desire. Thanks be to God for His loving-kindness. Amen.

Sixth Sunday After Pentecost

Our God has made for us a path in which to walk. In His will there is order and purpose. He has proclaimed and demonstrated eternal truth through the lips and lives of His children. He has given meaning to life, goal and objective to this existence. Therein is the answer to our inner needs, the fulfillment of our deepest longings. These things are more precious and of greater value than anything we could ever experience or even dare to imagine. This is the God whom we worship. We offer our praises to Him today. Amen.

Seventh Sunday After Pentecost

We have come to worship our God. We look to Him as our chief Counselor. Even in the darkest of nights He is ready to teach and guide us. We need only to recognize His presence. Because He continually surrounds us, we shall not lose our way. He does show us the paths we must take. Within His all-embracing presence there is genuine fulfillment. In our relationship with Him we discover incomparable and eternal joy. Accept, O Lord, the praises that pour forth from our lips today. Amen.

Eighth Sunday After Pentecost

Our everlasting God is a loving God. He knows all about our inner fears and doubts. He holds us back from the brink of destruction. He makes it possible for us to sing His praises and to rejoice in His deliverance. Ungodly nations sink in their own sewage. Men who promote evil snare themselves in their own nets. But those who recognize their need of God shall be found by Him, and they shall spend eternity praising Him. Amen.

Ninth Sunday After Pentecost

Our God will not forever remain silent. His voice like thunder will drown out the foolish boasts of His unfaithful creatures. "The maligned and the deprived have suffered long enough," He will say. "I will rise to their defense and grant them my protection." And what God promises, He will do. Keep us, O God, from the vile compromises and the rank complacency of this generation. As we walk in Your course for our lives, may our praises ascend continually to You. Amen.

Tenth Sunday After Pentecost

Where should we look for help in our need? To the majestic mountain peaks that probe our skies or the giants of industry that hem in our cities? To the satellites that circle our world or to the computers that store up our knowledge? The answer to our problems, the fulfillment of our needs must come from God Himself, from Him who created the skies and the mountains and man to dwell in their midst. This is the God whom we worship today. Amen.

Eleventh Sunday After Pentecost

Can there be any God but this God that we love? He surrounds us with His strength and clothes us with His grace. He puts into our hands gifts to relay to others. He entrusts us with tasks far beyond our human abilities and enables us to carry them out. He makes us His sons and daughters and commissions and empowers us to accomplish His purposes amongst the peoples of this world. This is our God; there is no other. Amen.

Twelfth Sunday After Pentecost

Our great God is our Refuge and our Strength. He is ever aware of our problems and concerned about our fears. Thus we have no business doubting Him even though the earth is convulsed in tragedy or its human masses threatened by nuclear annihilation. Nations will destroy each other; civilizations will perish; the earth itself may one day become a smoking cinder. Yet God's eternal plan is not canceled out by the whims of men or the freakish accidents of nature. God is here amongst us; He continues to be our Refuge and our Strength. Amen.

Thirteenth Sunday After Pentecost

It is in the grace and strength that our God grants that His servants find reason for celebration. He has truly fulfilled our innermost longings. He has responded to our deepest needs. We asked for security, and He encompassed us with love. We looked to Him for life, and He granted us life eternal. We sought for identity, and He adopted us as His sons and daughters. Whatever is of value and worth in our lives has come by way of His rich blessings. Our hearts are glad in the realization of His eternal presence. Amen.

Fourteenth Sunday After Pentecost

We know that our God stands by His own, that our failures do not stay His loving hand, that He can transform them into victories. Men about us will put their trust in rockets and computers; but such will fail to solve the real problems of their lives. It is only in the name of God that we who fail can find the grace to rise again. This is the God whom we praise today. May our mouths never cease to proclaim His majesty. Amen.

Fifteenth Sunday After Pentecost

As a desert wanderer longs for springs of cool water, so our thirsty souls reach out for our God. How we long for a deeper sense of His presence, for the kind of faith that will embrace Him without fear or doubt! We come to renew our faith in our God, to shout His praises even when we don't feel His presence, for truly He is our God and He is our Help and our Hope. Amen.

Sixteenth Sunday After Pentecost

The love of our God is beyond comprehension. It is no wonder that we reach incessantly for it and find security within it. Within the love of our Lord is the answer to our needs and the fulfillment of our desires. Continue, O God, to pour out Your saving love upon those who follow You. Do not allow the arrogance and infidelity of the godless to deter us from Your course for our lives. Accept our praises, O God, for we are Your children and Your servants. Amen.

Seventeenth Sunday After Pentecost

Even when we are beaten down by depression and ensnared by our weaknesses and frailties and our own lust threatens to devour us, our God is gracious and He will not let us go. We need to repeatedly renew our faith in our God, to walk in obedience to His will, to offer our lives as a continual thankoffering to Him. May God be praised forever. Amen.

Eighteenth Sunday After Pentecost

Like a thirsty child reaching for a drink of water, we grasp for our God. And we have found Him. We sense His hold presence in the worship service; and in the hour of prayer we feel that He is near. We realize now that His love for us is far better than life itself. Our hearts are full of joy and contentment. Our mouths are filled with praises for our God. Amen.

Nineteenth Sunday After Pentecost

We take comfort in the everlastingness of our God. He who outlives the seasons and the centuries, who has blessed the saints of the past, can also care for His servants in this fearful hour. For His years have no end, nor do the destinies of those who trust in Him. Great is our God, and we shall love and serve and worship Him forever. Amen.

Twentieth Sunday After Pentecost

We have failed because we expect too much of ourselves. We have fallen because we focused too much on success and have reckoned too little with our own humanity. It is time that we still our restless hearts and quiet our overambitious spirits. It is far better that we center our aspirations on God and His will for our lives. We have come to worship our God, for He is our Hope and our Salvation. Amen.

Twenty-first Sunday After Pentecost

How great and all-powerful is our God! The quaking of the earth, the shaking of the mountains, the blackness of the night, the beauty of the heavens, the lightning that criss-crosses our skies, the oceans that lash against our shores—these and much more bear witness to the majesty of our God. And this is the God who is concerned about us. Praise God! Amen.

Twenty-second Sunday After Pentecost

Let us give credit to whom credit is due? God is alive, and He deserves our perpetual praises. There is reason for rejoicing. There is a God to worship and love. His beauty is manifest in the skies and the forests. His power is represented in the sweep of the ocean. His majesty is portrayed in the gigantic bodies suspended in our universe. The wind and the rain, lightning and thunder, the creatures that inhabit our land: all this comes from God's hand. So let us give credit to whom credit is due! Let us rejoice in the God who blesses us! Let us seek His grace to serve Him by serving others with the abundance that He bestows upon us! Amen.

Twenty-third Sunday After Pentecost

Our loving God continues to preserve and to renew the world about us. His plans for His world and its inhabitants are not obliterated by the foolishness of men. His truth is not blotted out by the lethargy or lies of His apathetic creatures. He abides in this world among those who relate to Him, who rely on His ever-present love. He delivers His children from the fear of death and through them spreads

His Word of life in this world. God's love is sure and everlasting. The hearts that are open to His love are filled with joy. We celebrate the presence of our God in our world today. Amen.

Twenty-fourth Sunday After Pentecost

We praise our God. Even in the midst of this world's wickedness we celebrate His majesty and power. He is here with us. He is here to save; He is here also to judge. Even while the godless trumpet their rebellion, He holds the world in the palm of His hand. His fainthearted servants need not be dismayed. Even the rebelliousness of His obstinate creatures only serve to further His purposes. Let us renew our relationship to our God, rededicate our lives to His objectives, and continue to celebrate His presence and His power in our world. Amen.

Twenty-fifth Sunday After Pentecost

How great is our God! He soars above our poor intellects like a snowcapped mountain over a sunbaked desert. He scatters the profound theories of wise men like leaves pushed around by a winter wind. He shatters the assembled might of world governments as an earthquake levels a city. He reaches down in tenderness to earth's poor creatures and draws them to Himself. How great is our God! Amen.

Twenty-sixth Sunday After Pentecost

How great and glorious is our God! From hour to hour, from day to day, our lives ought to overflow with praise and gratitude. He creates beauty out of the dust of our fallen natures. Out of the ashes of our failures He brings forth meaning and purpose. He exalts the humble and enriches the poor. He transforms our weaknesses into channels of strength. Our emptiness becomes a vessel of His fullness, our spiritual poverty the basis for His eternal grace. But this is all God's doing, not ours. How great and glorious is our God! Amen.

Twenty-seventh Sunday After Pentecost

God is here; God is now! It is a time for celebration! The elements about us reflect His majesty. The roaring sea and all that inhabits it, the wind tha bends the trees, the creatures that fill the air and land, the mountains that probe our skies, the rivers and lakes that slake our thirst, the great planets and stars that light up our night: all these reveal the beauty and splendor of God. Wherever one turns, God's power is manifested; God's presence is made apparent. Let us celebrate His presence in our world today. Amen.

Last Sunday After Pentecost (Christ the King)

How great is our God, and how we love to sing His praises! Whereas we are often frightened when we think about the future and confused and disturbed by the rapidly changing events about us, our hearts are secured and made glad when we remember how He has cared for us throughout the past. When we were brought forth from our mother's womb, God's hand was upon us. Through parents and people who cared, He loved and sheltered us and set us upon His course for our lives. Through illness and accident our God has sustained us. Around pitfalls and precipices He has safely led us. We need never be afraid, no matter how uncertain may be the months or the years ahead of us. How great is our God as He is revealed through Christ our King, and how we love to sing His praises! Amen.

ALTERNATE
AND SPECIAL INTROITS

1

Our loving God is not looking for genius. He does not require great talents. He is not charmed by our panic-ridden activity. He simply asks for our faith and our obedience. It is when we turn from self-seeking to embrace His will for our lives that we discover serenity and security. It is thus that we come to our God today—to believe Him, to serve Him, and to praise Him. Amen.

2

We cannot find peace or security until we lose ourselves in something or someone that is greater than we are. It is thus that we seek to be drawn more deeply into the life and purposes of our God. Only then will we find shelter from the tempests of this fearful and uncertain existence. Only then will we be able to sing the praises of our God. Amen.

3

The earth continues to receive the abundance that God pours upon it. His blessings are all about us. May every mountain and valley, plain and forest, may every city street with its teeming apartments and sprawling suburbs echo with the praises of the children of God. Amen.

4

Our loving God does care for us, and He will fight with us against the enemies of our souls. Whether we be coming or going, He knows the course we take and He will go before us. Our times are in His hands. Praises be to our God. Amen.

5

We are exceedingly grateful to our God, for He has heard our cries and complaints and He has responded with mercy and strength. Now our lives are overflowing with thanksgiving; our mouths are filled with praises. Thanks be to our God. Amen.

6

Our Lord has not always shielded us from the pains of trouble or the ravages of conflict, but He has kept us even in the midst of sorrow and suffering. He has taken our side against the enemies of our souls, and He will not allow them to destroy us. Thus we know that He will fulfill His purposes for our lives. His love and mercy are everlasting. Praises be to our God! Amen.

7

We turn our thoughts toward our God. He has heard us before, and He has responded to our cries. Even amidst the frustrating activity and the crowded streets of the great city He can hear the cries of His lonely children. Our God delivers us from our prisons of loneliness. He turns our cries of distress into proclamations of joy. Praises be to our God! Amen.

8

We have come to praise our God. We know that He is in our midst, that He is aware of the fears and apprehensions of His beloved children. He may not always rid us of our fears; He does promise to face them with us, to make them stepping-stones to faith, to use them to draw us closer to Himself. We need not worry about the distortions of this world. We need to be aware that God is here and allow Him through us to reveal Himself to His world about us. Let us pour out our praises to our God! Amen.

9

Our God has indeed been good to us. He has prospered our land. He has opened His heart to us in love. He has forgiven us our sins and adopted us as His children. He touches us with joy and peace. He gives us what is good and prospers us with gifts from His hand. We know that He will never turn away from us. He is holy and just. He loves His children and guides them in His course for their lives. Thanks be to our God. Amen.

10

God is here; God is now! With voice and musical instruments, with lovely melodies and joyful sounds, let us proclaim the glory of our God. Let us fill our homes and sanctuaries, our halls of learning, our factories and marketplaces, even the streets of our city, with sounds of celebration! God is here; God is now! Amen.

11

Our hearts are full of joy today. We reach almost frantically for the sounds that might express that joy, the words that would proclaim the exuberance that we feel in this hour. We are heavy with praise, and we must express it lest we succumb to it. Our great God has marched into our jungle of despair and made a path for us to walk in once more. He sliced through our confusion and gave orders and motivation to our purposeless gropings. We rejoice in our powerful and ever-present God. Amen.

12

As the Word of our God is clear for those who would follow Him, so are His promises assured for that nation that will worship and serve Him. The enemies that threaten us and the problems that beset us can be absolved only in our returning to our God and in allowing Him to guide us and through us to bless the world about us. We seek the help of our God in restoring our great nation to those roots from which we came. Amen.

13

It may not always be apparent, but God does reign over our world. He rules in majesty and might, and no philosophy or power can cast Him from His throne. He allows us to cross up His purposes—even to destroy His visible creation about us. But His place and His reign are eternally secure. And they are secure who put their trust in Him, who live by His precepts, and who follow His course for their lives. This is the God that we worship today. This is the God whom we love and serve. Amen.

14

We shall begin this day with singing. Whether we feel like it or not, we shall make glad sounds and compel our tongues to articulate words of thanksgiving and praise. It is because God is with us. This world and we who live in it are in His hands. He loves us. He has adopted us as His children. We belong to Him forever. So let us begin this day with singing whether we feel like it or not. Then we may end this day with praises, because we know—and may even feel—that we shall forever be the objects of God's concern and the children of His love. Amen.

15

The Lord does reign over this world! Even when the earth quakes and the fires rage through the canyons and floods inundate the lowlands and men and their creations are laid low, God is Lord and Master over all the earth. Even when men turn against one another and nations are engaged in war, and violence and injustice are heaped upon His creatures, God is Lord and Master over all the earth. Our God relates to those who call upon Him. The priests and prophets of history heard His voice and followed in His course for their lives. His servants and disciples of this hour sense His presence and communicate His love and grace to those who reach out for Him. The Lord does reign over this world! He is Lord and Master over all the earth! Amen.

16

O Lord, how great and all-powerful You are! And how beautiful is the world You created for our habitation! Even before man was brought forth from the dust, You prepared for him a place in which to live and grow. And everything man saw about him reflected the beauty and power of the living God. O Lord, how great and all-powerful You are! And how beautiful is the world You created for our habitation! Amen.

17

We praise our God today! How exciting it is to be His sons and daughters! Our God is loving and patient. Even when we fail Him, He never fails to love and care for us. He never ceases to pursue us, to draw us back into His circle of love, and to carry out His purposes even through the failures and defeats of our lives. We praise our God today! We pray that He may find pleasure in our love for Him. Amen.

18

Our hearts are glad today, O God, and we are determined to serve You. We celebrate Your presence. We glory in Your love for us. We sing Your praises, and we desire to proclaim Your loving concern to all men and women about us. We know to whom we belong, and we know where we are going. We know that You are our Lord and that You will accompany us as we walk the streets of the city and mingle with its groping inhabitants. We pray, O Lord, that You will use us, and through our fumbling efforts touch others about us with Your healing and love. Our hearts are glad today, O God. Amen.

19

We come to praise You, O Lord, because You love us even when we fail to respond in loving obedience. Whereas we cannot comprehend You, You do understand us; and You continue to hold us within Your loving embrace. While we fall short of our sincere intentions to abide within Your will for us, Your promises are eternally secure; and you tenderly and patiently rekindle the fires within us and empower us to do that which we cannot do by ourselves. We have come to praise You, God. Amen.

20

How good it is to enter the sanctuary of the Lord! We know that God is not confined within man's four-walled creations, nor is He attached to altars and symbols. And yet, in the beauty and quietness of God's house we find His presence real and fulfilling. We rejoice as we enter His sanctuary and mingle with those who honor His name and seek His grace. There, shielded from the screaming tensions and ear-splitting sounds of the city, in the company of those who love one another, we happily open our hearts to the loving mercy of God. Amen.

21

Let us begin this day by rejoicing! Let us acknowledge our Lord's love and concern and allow our bodies to break forth into happy hilarity! Let us give our nerves and muscles the healthy exercise of laughter! The Lord has done such wonderful things in our midst; let us be glad! Amen.

22

We thank our eternal God for all these things that reveal His love: for the heavens that cover us, the earth beneath our feet, the sun in the day and the stars of the night, for the snow and the rains and the rivers and the lakes, for mountains and valleys and trees and flowers. We thank our eternal God. Amen.

23

We thank our eternal God for those people who demonstrate His love: for priests and prophets and apostles and ministers, for doctors and teachers and mothers and fathers and painters and musicians and writers and farmers and laborers and clerks, for those men and women who accepted His love and who dedicated their lives to loving their fellow persons. We thank our eternal God for choosing us to be His people, for calling us and equipping us to communicate His love to our world about us. We thank our eternal God. Amen.

24

How grateful we are to our God for our great country and for the blessings that He has poured out upon our land! How concerned we are lest our very nation may become our god and that we worship the gifts rather than the Giver! We pray, O God, that our nation be restored to Your objectives and that Your children who abide in this land dedicate their lives to You and Your purposes throughout the world. Amen.

25

How good it is to celebrate God's presence and to sing His praises throughout each day! We celebrate what He has done for man through history: His creation of our world and the sun and the moon and the unnumbered stars that light up our universe, His creatures that swim and crawl and walk and fly upon our planet, His children destined to enjoy these great gifts about them. How good it is to celebrate God's presence and to sing His praises throughout each day! Amen.

26

Our God does take note of those in conflict. He considers the godless and the arrogant. He is still Lord over all the world. He hears the cries of those who love Him. He is perpetually concerned about their needs. He will enable them to stand up against the oppressions and pains of this life. How great is our God! Amen.

27

How beautiful is the world our God created for our habitation! There was clean air. Pure water from snowcapped mountains flowed through green valleys and gathered together to become great lakes. The skies shone with a million lights. The land brought forth flowers and fruits to delight the eye and palate of God's creatures. And every part of the land and the waters that covered the land and the skies that looked down upon the land were filled with uncountable forms of life, and the world was vibrant and alive. How beautiful is the world our God created for our habitation! Amen.

10-101

```
BX          Brandt, Leslie F
8067
.I57          Contemporary
B7          introits for the
            revised Church
            calendar
```

```
BX          Brandt, Leslie F
8067
.I57          Contemporary
B7          introits for the
            revised Church
            calendar
```

DATE	ISSUED TO
MAR 2 0 1984	T. Voss 50¢

Concordia College Library
Bronxville NY 10708

23-520-002